Changing Climate

Jen Green

Chrysalis Children's Books

First published in the UK in 2003 by
Chrysalis Children's Books
An imprint of Chrysalis Books Group Plc
The Chrysalis Building, Bramley Road,
London W10 6SP

ISBN 1 84138 713 4

British Library Cataloguing in Publication Data for
this book is available from the British Library.

Editorial Manager: Joyce Bentley
Picture Researcher: Aline Morley
Produced by Tall Tree Ltd
Designer: Ed Simkins
Editor: Kate Phelps
Consultant: Michael Rand

Printed in China

Some of the more unfamiliar words used in this book
are explained in the glossary on page 31.

Photo Credits:
Front Cover(main), G. Wiltsie-Peter Arnold, inc./Still
Pictures; front cover(clockwise from top left), Klaus
Andrews/Still Pictures; Angela Hampton/Ecoscene;
Mark Edwards/Still Pictures; Mark Edwards/Still
Pictures; 1, Claude Charlier/Corbis; 2, NASA/Science
Photo Library; 4, G. Wiltsie-Peter Arnold, inc./Still
Pictures; 5(t), Martin Jones/Ecoscene; 5(b), Mark
Edwards/Still Pictures; 6, Royalty Free/Corbis; 7,
Angela Hampton/Ecoscene; 8, Roland Seitre/Still
Pictures; 9(t), Corbis-Sygma; 9(b), Hulton-Archive; 10,
Galen Rowell/Still Pictures; 11(t), M. Sewell-Peter
Arnold, inc./Still Pictures; 11(b), Andrew
Brown/Ecoscene; 13(t), Andrew Brown/Ecoscene;
13(b), Chin Ki Au/UNEP/Still Pictures; 14, Klaus
Andrews/Still Pictures; 15(t), Dylan Garcia/Still
Pictures; 15(b), Nigel Dickinson/Still Pictures; 16,
Graham Neden/Ecoscene; 17(t), Tony Wharton/FLPA;
17(b), Daniel Heuclin/Still Pictures; 18, Mark
Edwards/Still Pictures; 19(t), Claude Charlier/Corbis;
19(b), FLPA; 20(both) Ecoscene; 21, Mark
Edwards/Still Pictures; 22, NASA/Science Photo
Library; 23(t), Michel Gunther/Still Pictures; 23(b),
Mark Edwards/Still Pictures; 24, Corbis; 25, Steve
Prezant/Corbis; 26, Mark Edwards/Still Pictures; 27(t),
Guy Stubbs/Ecoscene; 27(b), Julia Baine/Still Pictures;
29, David Drain/Still Pictures; 30, Mark Edwards/Still
Pictures; 31, Angela Hampton/Ecoscene; back cover,
NASA/Science Photo Library.

Contents

The climate today

Climate is the regular weather pattern in a particular area. Today, climate is in the news because climate patterns are changing all over the world. What's more, scientists believe that these changes are happening because of what people are doing to the planet.

Earth is slowly getting warmer. This general rise in temperature is called global warming. The change is mostly caused by humans. As we burn fuels, such as coal and petrol, our cities, factories and cars give off fumes that pollute the atmosphere. This pollution is changing our climate.

◀ *Long periods of dry weather, called droughts, are increasingly common in the world today. This is due to global warming.*

A warmer climate will bring new dangers in the form of wild weather, such as storms and floods. World leaders are now working to slow down global warming and limit the dangers. We can all help by reducing the pollution given off by our homes and cars.

▲ *Global warming is bringing stormier weather to many parts of the world.*

CLOSE TO HOME

A layer of ozone gas high in the atmosphere helps screen us from the Sun's rays, which can burn our skin. Recently, this layer has been getting thinner. This means it is very important to put on suntan lotion to protect your skin from the Sun.

Weather and climate

In many parts of the world, the weather changes from day to day. Climate is a broader picture of the average weather conditions in an area measured over many years. Both weather and climate affect our daily lives.

All the different weather conditions we experience are caused by the Sun heating different parts of Earth more or less strongly. These differences make masses of warm and cool air move from one place to another, producing winds that bring storms, rain or snow.

▼ Oceans also affect climate. The sea heats up more slowly than the land but also cools down more slowly. This means that places by the sea are generally mild.

▼ Near the Equator, the Sun's rays are concentrated on a smaller area. Closer to the poles, the rays are spread over a wider area and also travel farther through the atmosphere, which makes them weaker.

Polar region

Temperate region

Sun's rays

Tropical region

Temperate region

Polar region

Earth's curving surface means that different parts of the world receive different amounts of heat from the Sun. The Sun beats down directly near the Equator, which makes the climate hot there. The Sun's rays shine more weakly in the polar regions, so it is much colder there.

CLOSE TO HOME

The seasons are regular, yearly changes that are most noticeable in temperate and polar regions. They happen because Earth tilts at an angle as it moves around the Sun. At any time of year, one half of our planet tilts towards the Sun and has summer. The other half tilts away from the Sun and has winter. Do the seasons bring many changes to the area where you live?

Measuring weather

What we call weather is really the air conditions at a particular place and time – whether the air is moist or dry, warm or cold, cloudy, windy or rainy. Scientists all over the world keep daily records of the weather.

Every day, weather stations on land and ships and buoys at sea collect information about the air conditions at ground or sea level. They measure temperature, wind speed, hours of sunshine and moisture. Weather balloons and planes measure conditions high in the atmosphere. Satellites circling above Earth track clouds and storms.

▼ *A polar scientist releases a weather balloon to gather information about conditions in the upper atmosphere.*

Detailed weather records have only been kept for about 150 years. However, we know quite a lot about past weather conditions because people have written about them in diaries. Old drawings and paintings also give clues about what the weather was like hundreds of years ago.

▲ *This weather expert is tracking the path of Hurricane Luis, which formed in 1995. Hurricanes are violent, whirling storms.*

LOOK CLOSER

Between about 1400 and 1900, Europe's climate was much colder than it is today. Writings and drawings like this one of the River Thames show that rivers and canals froze over regularly in winter. Frost fairs were held on the ice. These waterways rarely freeze today.

Climate patterns

Earth's climate does not stay exactly the same but has changed over the ages. For millions of years, it has regularly got colder and then warmer. These changes happen because Earth's orbit wobbles slightly as it goes round the Sun.

In the distant past, during periods we call ice ages, the temperature was several degrees colder than it is now. Ice covered much of the land in the temperate regions, as well as at the poles.

▼ Pine trees like this one can live for 4000 years. Scientists learn about the climate long ago by taking tiny samples from the tree trunks.

► *Scientists take samples from ice buried deep in the polar regions to learn about what the climate was like when the ice formed.*

Scientists find out about ice ages and climate change by studying ice buried deep in the polar regions. They also study trees. Every year, trees grow more quickly in summer. Their trunks grow wider as they add a new ring of woody growth under the bark. The widest growth rings occur in years of warm, wet weather. Scientists study old trees to learn about the climate hundreds, or even thousands, of years ago.

CLOSE TO HOME

Find a tree that has been cut down and carefully count the growth rings. Each ring is a year in the life of the tree, so you can tell how old it was when it was cut down. Are some rings more widely spaced than others? What does that mean?

The Greenhouse Effect

Earth's atmosphere is a blanket of gases surrounding the planet. The main gases in the atmosphere are nitrogen and oxygen. There are also small amounts of other gases that are important because they trap the Sun's heat.

In sunny weather, the glass in a greenhouse allows sunlight through and then traps the heat so it is warmer inside than outside. In Earth's atmosphere, certain gases, including carbon dioxide and methane, trap the Sun's heat in a similar way. They are known as greenhouse gases, and the warming they cause is called the Greenhouse Effect.

▼ Greenhouse gases in the atmosphere act as a heat barrier. Heat rising from Earth's surface is trapped by the barrier and returns to Earth to warm it.

Sun

Heat that escapes Earth's atmosphere

Heat

Layer of greenhouse gases in the atmosphere

Trapped heat

Earth's surface

Methane is a gas given off by swamps and also by grazing animals, such as cows, as they digest their food. Soggy rice fields also release methane. Rice is grown in vast quantities all over the world, including India and China (shown here). This contributes to the Greenhouse Effect.

In the past, the greenhouse gases have trapped just enough heat to allow nature to flourish on our planet. It is a delicate balancing act. Now people are disturbing the balance by polluting Earth.

◀ *Plants like these trees absorb carbon dioxide and give off oxygen. Animals breathe in oxygen and breathe out carbon dioxide.*

Upsetting the balance

For millions of years, the gases in the atmosphere have trapped just enough heat to warm our planet. People are now adding more and more greenhouse gases, which is causing temperatures to rise.

Carbon dioxide is the main greenhouse gas that people are adding to the atmosphere. We are doing this by burning fuels called fossil fuels – coal, oil and natural gas. These fuels are burned in power stations to make electricity, which is used in our homes, offices and factories to run all kinds of machines.

► *Factories and power stations release huge amounts of carbon dioxide and other greenhouse gases as they burn fossil fuels.*

Cars, lorries, planes and many trains also run on fossil fuels and release carbon dioxide. Rich countries, such as the United States and Britain, release far more carbon dioxide than poorer countries. This is because people in rich countries rely on cars and other machines, such as cookers and computers, to make life more comfortable.

◀ As cars burn diesel and petrol, they give off a mixture of polluting gases.

LOOK CLOSER

The cutting down of forests, particularly tropical rainforests, is also contributing to the rising levels of carbon dioxide in the air. When trees are burned to clear forests, they release carbon dioxide. Once they are gone, they can no longer absorb carbon dioxide. Huge areas of forests are destroyed each year.

Warming world

The atmosphere now contains one-third more carbon dioxide than it did 200 years ago. Higher levels of greenhouse gases are already causing global warming to take place.

In the last 50 years, experts believe that temperatures have already risen by 0.5°C. This may not sound much, but even a tiny rise can have a big effect. During the last Ice Age, the climate was only 4°C colder than it is now. Then our planet got much warmer. Now experts fear that temperatures may rise fairly fast.

◄ Experts think that global warming is starting to melt the ice packs covering the polar regions.

◀ *Icy glaciers high on mountains are also melting. Many glaciers are now only half the size they were 150 years ago. Some have disappeared completely.*

Weather records show that the 1990s were the hottest decade (ten-year period) for the last 150 years. Warmer weather will affect not only humans, but all living things. Each type of animal and plant is suited to live in a particular place on Earth. If the conditions change in one place, the animals and plants that live there must change, too, or die out.

CLOSE TO HOME

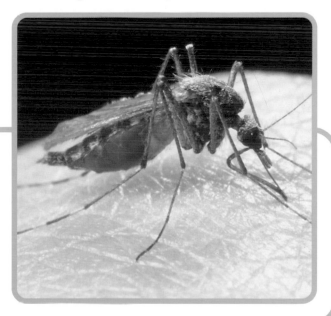

Warmer weather may actually suit some animals that people view as pests. Mosquitoes, shown here, are biting insects that can carry the deadly disease malaria. The malaria-carrying types usually live in tropical countries, but now global warming may be helping them spread to cooler places such as Europe.

Wild weather

Many experts now believe that global warming is starting to affect the world's weather. Violent storms are becoming more common throughout the world. Heatwaves, droughts and floods are striking more often, too.

The world's climate patterns have been disturbed by global warming. Some areas are becoming drier. Other regions are much wetter. In some places, heavy rain swells the water in rivers, which then burst their banks to flood the surrounding land.

▼ When drought strikes, water becomes scarce. This pump provides a village in Africa with its only supply of water.

Hurricanes and cyclones are powerful storms that form over warm oceans. When they reach land, they can wreck whole towns. In 1988, Hurricane Gilbert struck the Caribbean, killing 300 people. In 1997, Hurricane Andrew caused the devastating damage shown here to Miami, United States. If the oceans get warmer, these deadly storms may become more common – and even more violent.

◄ In 1993, the Mississippi River in the United States flooded a huge area of land. These floods are becoming more frequent as temperatures rise.

Hot, dry regions, such as Africa and Australia, seem to be getting even hotter and drier. In Australia, dry weather has sparked huge forest fires. In North Africa, the Sahara Desert is getting bigger. Some farming areas have now become too dry to grow crops.

Future dangers

Over the next century, global warming is also likely to bring other dangers. It may cause the oceans to expand, which will make sea levels rise. This will bring the danger of flooding to many areas. It may also affect ocean currents.

Warm water expands to take up more space than cooler water. This means that sea levels will rise as the oceans get warmer. Global warming is likely to melt the ice in the polar regions. The melting ice will also swell the seas. If coasts flood, millions of people worldwide will be made homeless.

► *Rising sea levels may threaten islands such as the Maldives in the Indian Ocean. These pictures of the same beach taken five years apart show the damage caused by rising sea levels. In the second picture, waves have washed away part of the sandy beach.*

Rising sea levels will bring the danger of flooding to coasts and low-lying regions worldwide. Large areas of low, flat countries such as Bangladesh and Holland may end up underwater. Global warming will also make it more difficult to grow crops in dry parts of countries such as the United States, China and India.

◀ *Drought stunts the growth of crops such as wheat, rice and millet.*
This African farmer is comparing healthy crops grown in a wet year with stunted crops grown during a drought.

LOOK CLOSER

The Gulf Stream is a current, or flow, of warm water in the Atlantic Ocean, which warms the shores of north-western Europe. It makes the climate there warmer than it would be without its warming effects. Ocean currents are driven by the Sun's heat. Scientists now fear that global warming may one day disturb currents such as the Gulf Stream, sending the warm water elsewhere.

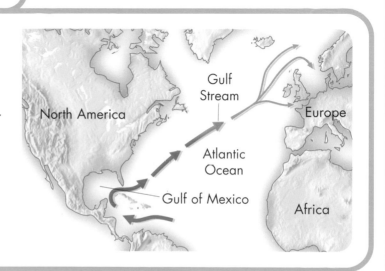

Ozone layer

Global warming is not the only modern climate problem. The layer of ozone gas high in the atmosphere, which screens Earth from harmful rays in sunlight, is also getting thinner. These harmful rays are called ultraviolet (UV) rays.

The ozone layer lies about 24 km above Earth's surface. Scientists believe that this layer has stayed the same for thousands of years, but recently it has got thinner. In the 1980s, scientists discovered that holes in the ozone layer had appeared over the Arctic and Antarctic. In the 1990s, the holes got bigger.

▲ In this computer-coloured satellite image from 1999, the darker blue colour shows the ozone hole over the Antarctic (darkest blue).

CLOSE TO HOME

At first, scientists were baffled about what was causing ozone loss. They soon found the answer. Chemicals called chlorofluorocarbons (CFCs) are the main troublemakers. These chemicals are used in the manufacture of aerosol-spray cans and some fridges. Foam packaging for fast foods, such as burgers, also contains CFCs.

▼ *Ozone loss means a higher risk of sunburn and even skin cancer for these sunbathers.*

Ozone loss allows harmful UV rays to reach Earth's surface. These rays burn human skin and can cause skin cancer. They can also cause other health problems such as eye cataracts. UV rays harm animals and plants both on land and in the sea.

Taking action

There is no doubt that harmful gases, such as carbon dioxide, CFCs and methane, are causing the problems of global warming and ozone loss. However, scientists and world leaders are now working together to tackle these climate problems and limit the damage they will cause.

Since the 1990s, several international conferences called Earth Summits have been organised. At these meetings, governments and climate experts have set targets to reduce the amount of carbon dioxide each country produces. However, some countries, such as the United States, are refusing to take steps to meet these targets.

▼ Turbines in a wind farm turn in the wind to make electricity without releasing greenhouse gases.

Fossil fuels that release carbon dioxide aren't the only energy sources we can use. There are other forms of energy that cause much less pollution. These include solar power, which uses energy from the Sun, and hydroelectric power, which uses energy from moving water. Our planet must use clean energy sources to reduce the damaging effects of global warming.

▼ *This map shows the amount of energy used by countries worldwide. Rich nations, such as the United States, produce far more pollution than poorer parts of the world.*

North America – 29.8%

Central and South America – 5.2%

Western Europe – 17.3%

Africa – 3.1%

Eastern Europe – 13.3%

Middle East – 5%

Asia – 19.3%

Japan, Australia and New Zealand – 7%

CLOSE TO HOME

Now that ozone loss has been tracked down to CFCs, most countries have decided to stop using these harmful chemicals. Ozone-friendly spray cans have replaced aerosols that use CFCs. Fast-food packaging and fridges are now being made using other chemicals.

How can we help?

There are many ways to help slow down the effects of global warming and reduce climate dangers. If everyone uses electricity more carefully, we can save energy and burn less fossil fuels. If every family saved even a little energy, it would have an enormous effect.

At home and at school, heating, lights, cooking and cleaning all use a lot of energy. Everyone can save energy by doing little things. For example, you can switch off lights and machines when they are not needed. In cold weather, you can put on warm clothes instead of turning the heating up. You can reuse plastic carrier bags for shopping and buy products that use less packaging.

▲ Children at the Earth Summit in Rio de Janeiro, Brazil, in 1992. People from countries around the world meet at these summits to discuss the future of the planet.

Tree-planting programmes help to restore woods and forests that have been cut down. We can help the atmosphere by planting a tree or by supporting organisations that are protecting the world's forests.

◀ *These school children in Africa are planting a tree to help replace lost forests.*

Travelling by car uses up a lot of fuel compared to travelling by public transport, because buses and trains carry more people. Can your family use the car less and walk, cycle or take the bus instead? Can you get to school using one of these methods or share a car ride with friends?

▲ *Cycling to school not only saves energy and helps the natural world, but it also keeps you fit!*

Climate projects

Find out more about temperature by doing a simple experiment with a thermometer.

Is climate change affecting the animals and plants where you live? Find out by keeping a nature diary.

INVESTIGATING TEMPERATURE
Learn about temperatures in your area using a thermometer.

1. On a sunny day, put a thermometer on a wall in the Sun. Check the temperature after half an hour. Now do the same in the shade. Make a note of the temperature difference.

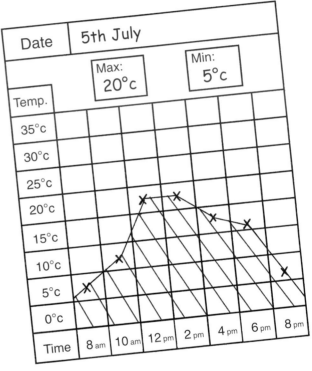

Date	5th July						
		Max: 20°c			Min: 5°c		
Temp.							
35°c							
30°c							
25°c							
20°c							
15°c							
10°c							
5°c							
0°c							
Time	8 am	10 am	12 pm	2 pm	4 pm	6 pm	8 pm

▲ *Record your findings on a graph in a notebook or on the computer. You could use the Internet or email a friend in another country to find out about temperatures in other parts of the world.*

2. Now try the thermometer inside a greenhouse on a sunny day with the windows closed. The raised temperature demonstrates how the greenhouse glass acts in the same way as greenhouse gases.

3. Keep a record of daily temperatures in the shade for a week each month to see how temperature varies throughout the year. Take readings at the same times each day, such as morning, noon and night. What does this tell you?

Annual nature diary

Find out how global warming is affecting animals and plants around you by keeping a diary about natural events over a couple of years.

Different types of plants bloom around the same time each year. For example, daffodils bloom in early spring. Warmer weather may now cause some plants to flower earlier. Record the weather and the date when you see different flowers appear.

Animals also follow annual cycles. For example, birds nest in spring, and some birds, such as geese and swallows, migrate (move) to warmer places for winter. Global warming may now cause some birds to nest earlier. Migrating birds may spend longer in their summer homes.

CAMPAIGN GROUPS

Friends of the Earth
26–28 Underwood Street
London N1 7JQ
Tel: 020 7490 1555
Website: www.foe.co.uk

Greenpeace
Canonbury Villas
London N1 2PN
Website: www.greenpeace.org

World Wildlife Fund (WWF)
www.wwf.org.uk

CLIMATE WEBSITES

US National Wildlife Federation: www.nwf.org/climate

US Environment Protection Agency:
www.epa.gov/globalwarming/kids

Other climate information sites:
www.education.noaa.gov/students.html

www.oneworld.net/penguin/global_warming/climate_home.html

www.coolclimate.org/climatechange.htm

US national weather service: www.crh.noaa.gov

UK weather service: www.weather.org.uk

Storm watch: www.stormwarn.com

Global Disaster Watch:
www.angelfire.com/on/predictions

Climate factfile

• Without the Greenhouse Effect, temperatures on Earth would be colder than in an ice age. Greenhouse gases make average temperatures on Earth over 30°C warmer than they would be otherwise.

• Since full weather records began in 1856, the six hottest years have all occurred since 1990.

• Every year, vehicles, industry, homes and burning forests pump nearly 7 billion tonnes of carbon dioxide into the atmosphere.

• Ozone, a bluish gas, is a form of oxygen. Unlike oxygen we breathe, ozone is poisonous.

• Sea levels are already rising by 1–2 mm each year. Scientists think sea levels may rise even faster in future – by 50–70 cm in the next 50 years.

• Holland is one country that is threatened by rising sea levels. One-third of the land there is below sea level. Walls called dykes keep the water at bay.

Glossary

Atmosphere
The layer of gases surrounding Earth. It protects us from the Sun's powerful rays.

Carbon dioxide
A gas in the atmosphere that plants absorb and animals breathe out. Carbon dioxide is a greenhouse gas.

Chlorofluorocarbons (CFCs)
Chemicals used in aerosol sprays and to make fridges and foam packaging. These chemicals damage the ozone layer.

Climate
The average pattern of weather in a region measured over many years.

Fossil fuels
Fuels such as coal, oil and natural gas. They are made of fossilised animals and plants that lived millions of years ago.

Global warming
A warming of the world's weather, caused by the increase of gases in the air that trap the Sun's heat. These gases, including carbon dioxide, are given off when fossil fuels are burned.

Greenhouse Effect
The warming effect caused by certain gases, called greenhouse gases, in the atmosphere. These gases trap more of the Sun's heat closer to Earth, where it warms the planet's surface.

Ice ages
Periods in Earth's history when the climate was colder than it is now.

Methane
A gas released from marshes, rice fields and cows' stomachs. Methane is a greenhouse gas.

Oxygen
A gas in the atmosphere that plants release and animals need to breathe.

Ozone layer
Ozone gas found high in the atmosphere that prevents harmful ultraviolet rays in sunlight from reaching Earth.

Pollution
Disturbing Earth's natural balance by releasing dirty chemicals. Pollution may affect the land, water or air.

Ultraviolet (UV) rays
Harmful rays in sunlight that burn human skin and can cause other health problems.

Index